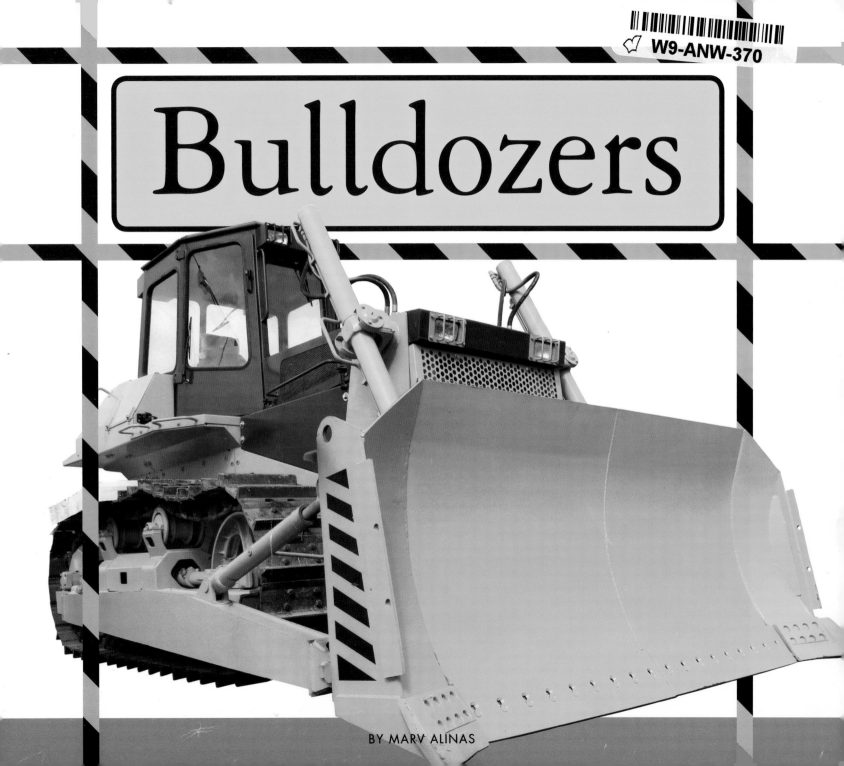

Bulldozers

BY MARV ALINAS

Published by The Child's World®
1980 Lookout Drive • Mankato, MN 56003-1705
800-599-READ • www.childsworld.com

Acknowledgments
The Child's World®: Mary Berendes, Publishing Director
The Design Lab: Design
Jody Jensen Shaffer: Editing
Pamela J. Mitsakos: Photo Research

Photos
arenaphotouk/123RF.com: 12; Art Konovalo/
Shutterstock.com: cover, 1; Bonita R. Cheshier/
Shutterstock.com: 19; FoxFoto/iStock.com: 20; Olivier
Le Queinec/BigStockPhoto.com: 15; ownway/iStock.
com: 8; Picsfive/Shutterstock.com: 7; smereka/
Shutterstock.com: 4; TFoxFoto/Shutterstock.com: 11;
TSpider/Shutterstock.com: 16

ISBN 9781623239626
LCCN 2013947248

Printed in the United States of America
Mankato, MN
November, 2013
PA02190

Contents

This bulldozer
is pushing dirt and rocks.

What are bulldozers?

Bulldozers are powerful earth-moving machines. They flatten bumpy ground. They push huge piles of dirt and rock. They break up hard ground, too.

How are bulldozers used?

Bulldozers are used for many jobs. They help people build roads and buildings. They push trees and brush out of the way. They move dirt and rock where they are needed. They even move trash at city dumps.

This bulldozer
is being used
at a city dump.

engine

crawler tracks

What are the parts of a bulldozer?

The bulldozer's body holds a big **engine**. The engine provides power that makes the bulldozer go. The bulldozer sits on wide metal belts. These belts are called **crawler tracks**. The tracks help the bulldozer move over bumpy ground.

The front of the bulldozer has a metal **blade**. The blade can be straight or curved. Metal arms move the blade up and down. The blade is used for pushing things. It is strong enough to push big piles of rock.

A bulldozer's blade
is made of heavy metal.

The ripper tools are heavy and powerful.

Many bulldozers have **rippers** on the back. These rippers have big metal claws. They help bulldozers break up rocky or hard ground. Some rippers have two or three claws.

Who drives a bulldozer?

The bulldozer's driver is called the **operator**. The operator sits in the **cab**. The cab has a seat and **controls**. The controls make the bulldozer move. The controls make the blade go up and down. They make the rippers go up and down, too.

The cab sits up high so the operator can see.

The crawler tracks can grip almost all types of ground.

How do bulldozers move?

A bulldozer crawls along on its moving metal tracks. The tracks can move forward or backward. They grip the ground. They also spread the bulldozer's weight. They keep the bulldozer from sinking in soft ground.

Bulldozers move slowly. They often go only about 6 miles (10 km) an hour. They are too slow and heavy to drive on streets. Trucks carry them from job to job.

A truck is taking this bulldozer to the next job.

OVERSIZE LOAD

These bulldozers are getting the ground ready for a highway.

Are bulldozers important?

People use bulldozers all over the world. They use them for all kinds of earthmoving jobs. Without bulldozers, these jobs would be hard to do. Bulldozers are very important!

GLOSSARY

blade (BLAYD) A blade is a part that is broad, flat, and usually thin. A bulldozer's blade pushes things.

cab (KAB) A machine's cab is the area where the operator sits.

controls (kun-TROHLZ) Controls are parts that people use to run a machine.

crawler tracks (KRAW-lur TRAKS) Crawler tracks are metal belts that some machines use for moving.

engine (EN-jun) An engine is a machine that makes something move.

operator (OP-ur-ay-tur) A machine's operator is the person who runs the machine.

rippers (RIP-purz) On bulldozers, rippers are strong metal parts with claws. The claws loosen hard dirt and rocks.

BOOKS

Askew, Amanda. *Bulldozers*. Toronto: Firefly Books, 2010.

Butterfield, Moira. *Look Inside Cross-Sections: Bulldozers*. New York: Dorling Kindersley, 1995.

Parent, Nancy. *The Bulldozer*. New York: Scholastic, 2003.

Teitelbaum, Michael. *If I Could Drive a Bulldozer!* New York: Scholastic, 2002.

WEB SITES

Visit our Web site for lots of links about bulldozers:
childsworld.com/links

Note to parents, teachers, and librarians: We routinely check our Web links to make sure they're safe, active sites—so encourage your readers to check them out!

INDEX

ABOUT THE AUTHOR

Marv Alinas has lived in Minnesota for over thirty years. When she's not reading or writing, Marv enjoys spending time with her dog and traveling to small river towns in northeastern Iowa and western Wisconsin.